LEADERSHIP HANDOVER

"Ensuring a smooth transition"

BY
Carol Sichembo

Target Audience: Leaders at all levels, including those transitioning into or out of leadership roles, HR professionals, and anyone involved in succession planning.

Overall Goal: Equip readers with the knowledge and tools to design and execute effective leadership handovers, minimizing disruption and maximizing success.

BOOK OUTLINE.

Chapter 1: The Importance of the Handover

- Why handovers matter: Inevitability of change, knowledge transfer, maintaining momentum, team morale
- The cost of a bad handover: Potential for confusion, delays, decreased productivity, employee dissatisfaction
- Benefits of a well-planned handover: Improved team performance, increased employee engagement, smoother integration of new leader

Chapter 2: Preparing for the Transition

- Initiating the handover process: Identifying the timeframe, setting clear expectations
- The role of the outgoing leader: Developing a handover plan, sharing knowledge, building relationships with the successor
- The role of the incoming leader: Demonstrating initiative, actively learning, asking questions
- The role of the organization: Providing resources and support, fostering a culture of collaboration.

Chapter 3: Key Elements of the Handover

- Defining the scope of the handover: Responsibilities, projects, team dynamics
- Knowledge transfer strategies: Documentation, meetings, mentoring, shadowing
- Communication strategies: Internal announcements, stakeholder engagement, open communication channels

Chapter 4: Challenges and How to Overcome Them

- Lack of time: Strategies for efficient knowledge transfer and prioritizing information
- Power dynamics: Managing egos and ensuring a smooth transfer of authority

- Resistance to change: Strategies for building buy-in and fostering a positive transition

Chapter 5: Successful Handovers: Case Studies

- Examples of effective leadership handovers in various contexts (business, religious, non-profit)
- Analysis of factors that contributed to success.

Chapter 6: Beyond the Handover: Building a Culture of Continuity

- Succession planning strategies: Identifying and developing future leaders
- Creating a learning organization: Encouraging knowledge sharing and continuous improvement
- The importance of building strong teams: Developing leadership skills across the organization.

Chapter 7: The Handover in Different Contexts

- Planned vs. Unplanned Transitions: Adapting your approach for unexpected leadership changes.
- Handovers in Mergers and Acquisitions: Managing integration and cultural differences.
- Handovers in Non-Profit Organizations: Considering unique challenges and best practices.

Chapter 8: Communication Strategies for Complex Handovers

- Managing sensitive information and difficult conversations.
- Building trust and transparency during the transition.
- Effective communication with stakeholders at all levels.

Chapter 9: The Long-Term Impact of Effective Handovers

- How successful handovers contribute to a culture of high performance.
- Measuring the success of your handover process.
- The impact on employee retention and satisfaction.

Chapter 10: The Future of Leadership Handovers

- Emerging trends and technologies in the leadership development landscape.
- The changing role of HR and talent management in handovers.
- Preparing for the future of successful leadership transitions

- **Conclusion:**

Chapter 1: The Importance of the Handover: Ensuring a Smooth Baton Pass

The leadership landscape is a dynamic one. Leaders emerge, inspire, and guide their teams to achieve great things. But even the most visionary leader eventually reaches a turning point. Retirement beckons, new opportunities arise, or life takes an unexpected turn. Here's where the true test of an organization's resilience lies: the leadership handover.

This transition period, often viewed as a necessary but cumbersome hurdle, holds immense significance. Done poorly, it can cripple momentum, erode morale, and leave the organization reeling. Done thoughtfully, however, a handover can be a catalyst for continued growth, fostering stability, and empowering the next generation of leadership.

The Peril of a Fumbled Baton:

Imagine a skilled conductor leading an orchestra through a stirring symphony. Each musician plays their part flawlessly, weaving a tapestry of sound that enthralls the audience. But then, abruptly, the conductor departs mid-movement. Without clear direction, the orchestra falls into discord[1]. Notes are missed, tempos clash, and the once harmonious music dissolves into chaos.

This analogy aptly illustrates the potential consequences of a botched leadership handover. Here's a closer look at the potential pitfalls:

- **Loss of Momentum:** Organizations operate in a competitive environment. A leadership vacuum creates uncertainty and stagnation, allowing competitors to gain an edge.

---
[1]

- **Knowledge Drain:** Departing leaders often possess a wealth of institutional knowledge. Without a proper transfer, this knowledge walks out the door, hindering the organization's ability to navigate complex projects or maintain crucial relationships.
- **Employee Morale Plummets:** A chaotic transition breeds anxiety and confusion among employees. Trust in leadership wanes, leading to disengagement and decreased productivity.
- **Stakeholder Relations Suffer:** Investors, clients, and other stakeholders rely on stability and direction. A messy leadership handover can erode trust, potentially damaging the organization's reputation.

These consequences highlight the critical need for a well-planned and executed handover process.

The Symphony of Success: A Seamless Transition

Thankfully, with proper planning and effort, a leadership handover can be a smooth and successful affair. Here are some key benefits that can be achieved:

- **Uninterrupted Progress:** A well-orchestrated handover minimizes disruption, allowing the organization to maintain its forward momentum without missing a beat.
- **Enhanced Knowledge Transfer:** A structured approach ensures the systematic transfer of critical knowledge and expertise from the outgoing leader to the incoming one.
- **Boosted Employee Morale:** A clear and transparent transition fosters trust and confidence within the team. Employees feel reassured that the organization is well-prepared for the future.
- **Strengthened Stakeholder Relationships:** A well-managed handover demonstrates the organization's stability and commitment to long-term

success. Investors and partners gain renewed confidence, solidifying the organization's reputation.

Beyond the Practical: The Human Element of Handovers

Leadership handovers often get bogged down in the practicalities – checklists, documents, and timelines. However, there's a crucial human element at play, one that fuels successful transitions. It's about a shared passion for the organization's mission, a respect for the legacy being passed on, and a genuine commitment to setting the new leader up for success.

Imagine a seasoned athlete passing the baton in a relay race. There's a mix of emotions – pride in past achievements, a touch of sadness at leaving the track, and most importantly, a fervent belief in the potential of the next runner. This same spirit of passion and dedication is essential for a successful leadership handover. When both the outgoing and incoming leaders approach the transition with a commitment to the organization's future, the baton is passed seamlessly, setting the stage for continued success.

Embracing the Inevitability of Change

Leadership transitions are not anomalies; they are an inherent part of any organization's lifecycle. By understanding the high cost of a botched handover and appreciating the symphony of success that can arise from a well-planned process, organizations can approach this critical juncture with purpose and passion. This book serves as your guide, providing the knowledge and tools to ensure a smooth and successful leadership handover, ultimately strengthening your organization's resilience and propelling it towards a bright future.

As the Zambian proverb says, "Imiti ikula ey mpanga" – "today's small trees are the forest of tomorrow." Just as young trees nurtured today will one day become the towering giants of the forest, a well-prepared incoming leader, supported by a smooth handover process, can ensure the organization's continued growth and success.

Imagine a seasoned athlete passing the baton in a relay race. There's a mix of emotions – pride in past achievements, a touch of sadness at leaving the track, and most importantly, a fervent belief in the potential of the next runner. This same spirit of passion and dedication is essential for a successful leadership handover. When both the outgoing and incoming leaders approach the transition with a commitment to the organization's.

Chapter 2: Preparing for the Transition.

Imagine a lush garden teeming with life. Vibrant flowers bloom, casting their fragrance on the air. But beneath the surface, a network of roots weaves silently, unseen yet vital. These roots, established with care, provide the foundation for growth, ensuring the garden's continued beauty long after the initial planting.

A successful leadership handover resembles this carefully nurtured garden. It's about laying the groundwork for a smooth transition, ensuring the organization thrives even as leadership changes hands. This chapter delves into the heart of handover preparation, a process driven not just by checklists and timelines, but by genuine care and foresight.

The Seeds of Success: Initiating the Handover with Open Hearts

Leadership handovers can feel daunting, a looming storm cloud on the horizon. But there's a simple truth often overlooked – a smooth handover doesn't just happen; it's nurtured. The seeds of success are sown when the organization recognizes the inevitability of change and chooses to embrace it proactively.

Imagine the outgoing leader not as someone departing, but as a seasoned gardener entrusting their prized roses to a new caretaker. Here, the focus shifts from loss to legacy, fostering a spirit of collaboration and knowledge sharing. The outgoing leader, with a heart filled with pride and a touch of melancholy, can ensure the new leader inherits not just responsibilities, but a deep understanding of the organization's soil – its history, values, and challenges.

Planting the Right Seeds: Identifying the Ideal Successor

Just as not every plant thrives in every garden, not every leader is a perfect fit for every organization. Selecting the right successor is a crucial component of handover preparation. This requires a keen eye for talent, a commitment to diversity, and a heart that recognizes potential. The focus should go beyond experience and qualifications. Look for someone who shares the organization's core values, who possesses a future-oriented mindset, and who inspires trust and confidence within the team. Imagine the excitement of discovering a young sapling with strong roots and vibrant leaves, hinting at the potential to blossom into a majestic tree.

Cultivating Growth: Fostering a Supportive Environment

Change can breed anxiety, and leadership handovers are no exception. The incoming leader might feel overwhelmed by the weight of expectation. The outgoing leader might struggle to let go. This is where the organization must step up, nurturing a supportive environment that allows for growth and collaboration.

Mentorship programs and knowledge-sharing initiatives can bridge the gap between the outgoing and incoming leader. Open communication channels and a culture of trust create a safe space for questions, concerns, and constructive feedback. Imagine the garden bathed in warm sunlight, each plant receiving the necessary nourishment to flourish.

The Heart of the Matter: Beyond Processes and Checklists

Leadership handover preparation goes beyond the practicalities of timelines and checklists. It's about a genuine commitment to the organization's future. It's about respecting the legacy of the outgoing leader while preparing the incoming one for success. It's about nurturing a spirit of collaboration and shared purpose.

Let's not forget the human element – the emotions, the hopes, and the anxieties that accompany change. By fostering open communication, empathy, and a shared vision for the future, we cultivate a fertile ground for a smooth leadership transition. Just as the roots of a plant connect it to the earth, a well-prepared handover connects the past, present, and future of an organization, ensuring its continued growth and success.

Leadership Handover in the Bible

The concept of a well-prepared leadership handover isn't a modern invention. It's a concept woven into the fabric of history, with lessons applicable even today. Take the story of Moses and Joshua from the Bible. Moses, a revered leader who guided the Israelites out of Egypt, faced a critical juncture in his journey. As his time neared its end, the responsibility of leading the Israelites into the Promised Land fell upon a chosen successor – Joshua.

Planting the Seeds of Leadership in Joshua.

Moses didn't simply announce Joshua as his successor and expect a smooth transition. He nurtured Joshua's leadership potential over an extended period. Here are some key parallels between Moses' actions and the principles of effective handover preparation in today's world:

- **Exposure and Experience:** Moses included Joshua in crucial decision-making processes. He allowed Joshua to witness firsthand the challenges and triumphs of leading the Israelites. This mirrors the importance of giving potential successors hands-on experience and exposure to leadership dynamics.
- **Mentorship and Knowledge Sharing:** The Bible describes Moses spending time with Joshua in the

"Tent of Meeting," a place of prayer and communion with God. This can be seen as a form of mentorship, where Moses imparted his wisdom and knowledge to Joshua. Similarly, organizations can facilitate mentorship programs to ensure smooth knowledge transfer between leaders.

- **Building Trust and Confidence:** The Israelites trusted Moses implicitly. By choosing Joshua and allowing him to take on leadership roles, Moses fostered trust and confidence in his successor among the people. This aligns with the importance of building public support for the incoming leader during a handover process.

From the Sands of Time to the Modern Boardroom

The story of Moses and Joshua offers valuable insights for leaders preparing for a handover in today's world. Here's how we can translate these ancient practices into practical steps:

- **Early Identification:** Identify potential successors early on, allowing them to gain experience and grow into their leadership roles.
- **Mentorship Programs:** Establish formal or informal mentorship programs where outgoing leaders can share their wisdom and expertise.
- **Succession Planning Workshops:** Organize workshops to equip potential successors with the skills and knowledge necessary for effective leadership.

By following these principles, organizations can cultivate a fertile ground for leadership succession, ensuring a smooth transition and continued success.

The Journey Continues: Cultivating Your Handover Garden

The story of Moses and Joshua serves as a reminder that leadership handover is not just about handing over responsibilities. It's about nurturing talent, fostering collaboration, and ensuring a seamless baton pass.

The following chapters will delve deeper into the practical aspects of handover preparation, equipping you with the tools and strategies to cultivate your own successful handover garden. Remember, with a little care and foresight, you can ensure that your organization continues to thrive, even as leadership changes hands.

Chapter 3: Key Elements of the Handover.

A successful leadership handover resembles a flawlessly conducted symphony. Each element – the meticulous preparation, the clear communication, the seamless collaboration – plays a crucial role in creating a harmonious and impactful performance. In this chapter, we delve into the key elements that orchestrate a smooth and successful leadership transition.

1. Early Planning and Announcement:

Proactive planning is the cornerstone of a successful handover. Don't wait until the outgoing leader is on the verge of departure to initiate the process. Ideally, the handover timeline should be established well in advance, allowing ample time for each stage. Here's what early planning entails:

- **Succession Planning Committee:** Establish a dedicated committee responsible for overseeing the handover process. This committee can comprise senior leaders, HR representatives, and potentially an external consultant with expertise in leadership transitions.
- **Defining the Handover Timeline:** Create a detailed timeline outlining key milestones, such as the official announcement of the handover, the completion of knowledge transfer activities, and the formal handover date.
- **Public Announcement:** Once the handover timeline is established, make a clear and timely announcement to all stakeholders, including employees, clients, and investors. This fosters transparency and minimizes uncertainty

2. Identifying and Selecting the Successor:

Choosing the right successor is paramount. Look beyond simply filling a vacant position; seek a leader who aligns with the organization's vision, possesses the necessary skills, and inspires confidence within the team. Here are some key considerations:

- **Competency and Experience:** The successor should possess the skills and experience required to navigate the organization's current challenges and future opportunities.
- **Leadership Style and Cultural Fit:** Consider how the new leader's leadership style aligns with the organization's culture. A smooth transition is more likely when the incoming leader can build upon the existing foundation.
- **Succession Development Programs:** Invest in leadership development programs to cultivate internal

talent and prepare potential successors for future leadership roles.

3. Knowledge Transfer: Bridging the Gap

A critical element of a successful handover is the systematic transfer of knowledge from the outgoing leader to the incoming one. This knowledge encompasses everything from the organization's history and strategic goals to industry trends and key client relationships. Here are some strategies to ensure effective knowledge transfer:

- **Mentorship Programs:** Pair the outgoing and incoming leader in a formal or informal mentorship program. This allows for focused knowledge sharing and fosters a collaborative handover environment.
- **Knowledge Transfer Documents:** Create comprehensive documents that capture the outgoing leader's knowledge and expertise. This may include

strategic plans, project summaries, and summaries of key client relationships.

- **Shadowing Opportunities:** Provide the incoming leader with opportunities to shadow the outgoing leader in meetings, presentations, and other key activities. This allows for firsthand observation and practical learning.

4. Communication is Key: Transparency and Collaboration

Effective communication is the lifeblood of a smooth handover. Here are some best practices to ensure clear and transparent communication throughout the process:

- **Open Communication Channels:** Establish clear communication channels for all stakeholders, allowing for questions, concerns, and feedback. Regular town halls, internal memos, and dedicated communication channels can facilitate this.

- **Consistent Messaging:** Maintain a consistent message about the handover process across all communication channels. This minimizes confusion and fosters trust among employees and external stakeholders.
- **Collaboration Between Incoming and Outgoing Leaders:** Encourage collaboration between the outgoing and incoming leaders. Joint appearances, team meetings, and co-authored communication pieces can showcase a unified approach to the transition.

5. Managing Stakeholders Through the Transition.

A successful handover requires managing the expectations and concerns of various stakeholders, including employees, clients, and investors.

- **Employee Engagement:** Address employee anxieties and concerns through clear communication, town halls, and Q&A sessions. Highlight the organization's commitment to stability and continued success.

- **Client Reassurance:** Proactively communicate the handover to clients and emphasize the continuity of service and expertise. Offer opportunities for the incoming leader to meet with key clients and establish rapport.
- **Investor Confidence:** Maintain open communication with investors throughout the handover process. Highlight the organization's robust succession planning and the incoming leader's qualifications.

The Conductor's Baton: Leading the Way to a Successful Handover

By orchestrating these key elements – early planning, strategic selection, knowledge transfer, open communication, and stakeholder management –

organizations can create a smooth and successful leadership handover. Such proactive planning ensures a seamless baton pass, guaranteeing the continued growth and success of the organization, even as leadership changes hands.

The story of Elijah blessing his successor, Elisha, is a powerful one that resonates today in many ways. Here are some connections you can make:

- **Mentorship and passing the torch:** In many fields, experienced individuals guide and prepare the next generation. We see this in professions, businesses being passed down through families, or even just teaching a friend a new skill.
- **Importance of legacy:** Elijah entrusts Elisha with carrying on his work. This is a reminder that we all have the opportunity to leave a positive impact and inspire others to continue our efforts.

- **Transition and change:** Even important roles eventually change hands. This is relevant in leadership changes, personal growth, or simply adapting to new situations.
- **Faith and calling:** In the biblical story, Elijah recognizes Elisha as chosen for a purpose. This can connect to finding your own path or purpose in life.

How you relate this story today depends on your specific situation. Think about what aspect resonates most with you and use it as inspiration.

Chapter 4: Challenges and How to Overcome Them.

A smooth handover is crucial for ensuring continuity, efficiency, and maintaining quality in any situation. Whether it's a project transitioning between teams, a shift change for medical professionals, or knowledge transfer during an employee departure, challenges can arise. Let's explore some common hurdles and strategies to overcome them:

Challenges:

- **Incomplete or Inaccurate Information:** Missing details, outdated information, or misunderstandings during the handover can lead to confusion and delays.
- **Lack of Communication:** Ineffective communication, either verbal or written, can leave the receiving party unclear about priorities, tasks, or potential issues.
- **Time Constraints:** Feeling rushed during a handover can lead to skipped information or a lack of opportunity to ask clarifying questions.
- **Knowledge Gaps:** The receiving party may lack the knowledge or experience necessary to handle the task or situation effectively.

- **Unclear Expectations:** Undefined expectations about roles, responsibilities, and deadlines can lead to frustration and wasted effort.
- **Resistance to Change:** People accustomed to a certain way of doing things may resist adopting new processes or procedures introduced during handover.

Strategies:

- **Standardized Handover Process:** Develop a structured approach to handover, including checklists, templates, and clear guidelines for information transfer.
- **Detailed Documentation:** Create comprehensive documentation outlining project details, procedures, current status, and any known issues.
- **Effective Communication:** Utilize a combination of clear verbal explanations, written documentation, and visual aids, allowing ample time for questions and clarification.

- **Knowledge Sharing:** Facilitate knowledge transfer through training sessions, mentoring, or shadowing opportunities for the receiving party.
- **Clearly Defined Expectations:** Set clear expectations regarding roles, responsibilities, deadlines, and success metrics before the handover is complete.
- **Embrace Change Management:** Address potential resistance to change by involving relevant parties in the development of the handover process and emphasizing the benefits of improvement.

Additional Tips:

- **Conduct Handover Meetings:** Organize dedicated meetings for handover discussions, allowing for in-depth discussions and clarification.
- **Utilize Technology:** Leverage project management tools, communication platforms, or

knowledge-sharing software to streamline the handover process.

- **Feedback and Post-Handover Support:** Gather feedback on the handover process to identify areas for improvement. Offer ongoing support to the receiving party after the official handover is complete.

By implementing these strategies, you can minimize the challenges associated with handover and ensure a smooth transition, ultimately leading to improved efficiency, quality, and overall success.

Political Handovers: A Balancing Act Between Continuity and Change.

Political transitions, or handovers, are a crucial yet often bumpy part of the democratic process. While continuity of governance is essential, the incoming administration also has the mandate to implement new policies and approaches. Here's a look at some key challenges in political handovers, using real-world examples:

Challenges:

- **Incomplete Information and Partisan Bias:** Outgoing administrations may be reluctant to share sensitive information or may present a biased picture of ongoing projects. This can hinder the incoming administration's ability to make informed decisions.
    - **Example:** The 2017 transition between the Obama and Trump administrations saw accusations of incomplete briefings on foreign policy matters and critical infrastructure projects.
- **Lack of Cooperation:** Outgoing administrations may be unwilling to cooperate with the incoming team, creating delays and hindering a smooth transition.
    - **Example:** The 2000 US election between George W. Bush and Al Gore resulted in a legal

battle that delayed the handover, impacting national security briefings and the preparation of the federal budget.

- **Knowledge Gaps and Staffing Challenges:** Political appointees often lack experience in government bureaucracy. Filling key positions with qualified personnel can take time, creating leadership vacuums.
    - **Example:** In India, following major election victories, new governments often face challenges in filling key cabinet positions with individuals with relevant experience, especially in crucial sectors like finance or defense.
- **Public Uncertainty and Market Volatility:** Uncertainties surrounding policy changes during a handover can lead to public anxiety and market volatility.
    - **Example:** The 2016 UK vote to leave the European Union (Brexit) caused significant uncertainty about the future of trade deals and

regulations, leading to fluctuations in the British pound and impacting businesses across Europe.

Strategies for a Successful Handover:

- **Standardized Handover Procedures:** Establishing clear guidelines for information transfer, personnel briefings, and transition planning can improve efficiency.
- **Dedicated Transition Teams:** Creating dedicated teams within outgoing and incoming administrations can facilitate communication and ensure a smooth knowledge transfer.
- **Non-Partisan Briefings:** Independent experts or career bureaucrats can provide objective information on ongoing projects and national security concerns.
- **Public Communication and Transparency:** Clear and consistent communication from both

administrations can help manage public expectations and minimize market volatility.

Examples of Successful Transitions:

- **South Africa (1994):** The transition from white minority rule to a multiracial democracy under Nelson Mandela was marked by extensive planning and cooperation between the outgoing and incoming administrations.
- **Ireland (2011):** Despite political differences, a smooth handover between the Fianna Fáil and Fine Gael parties ensured policy continuity during a period of economic crisis.

By acknowledging the challenges and implementing effective strategies, political actors can work together to ensure a smooth handover that minimizes disruption and fosters a stable environment for the continuation of good governance.

Chapter 5: Successful Handovers: Case Studies

The road to a smooth handover can be fraught with challenges, but the rewards are substantial – continuity, efficiency, and a strong foundation for future success. This chapter explores real-world examples of successful handovers across different industries, highlighting the strategies that made them work.

Case Study 1: Tech Startup - Scaling Up for Growth

Company: Acme Innovations, a young tech company developing a revolutionary new fitness tracker.

Handover Situation: The company secured a significant round of funding, necessitating a leadership transition from the founder, a visionary innovator, to a CEO with strong business management experience.

Challenges:

- **Maintaining Innovation Culture:** Balancing the need for more structured processes with the company's core innovative spirit.
- **Knowledge Transfer:** Ensuring smooth knowledge transfer between the founder and the new CEO regarding product development and ongoing partnerships.
- **Employee Morale:** Addressing potential anxieties amongst employees about changing leadership and company culture.

Strategies for Success:

- **Phased Handover:** The founder gradually transitioned responsibilities over a period of months, providing mentorship and guidance to the new CEO.
- **Joint Leadership:** The founder and CEO initially worked together, allowing for a seamless blend of innovation and business acumen.
- **Open Communication:** Regular company-wide meetings were held to address concerns, share the vision for the future, and reaffirm the company's commitment to innovation.

Result: Acme Innovations successfully scaled its operations while maintaining its innovative spirit. The new CEO leveraged the founder's product knowledge and established strong relationships with investors and partners. Employee morale remained high as the company transitioned to a new phase of growth.

Case Study 2: Manufacturing Giant - Embracing Automation

Company: Global Steel Inc., a leading manufacturer facing increasing competition and rising production costs.

Handover Situation: The company's long-time CEO, known for his focus on traditional manufacturing methods, was retiring. The new CEO was a strong advocate for automation and technological advancements.

Challenges:

- **Resistance to Change:** Long-time employees accustomed to traditional methods might resist the introduction of new technologies.

- **Reskilling Workforce:** The shift towards automation would require training existing employees in new skills.
- **Managing Costs:** Balancing the upfront investment in automation with maintaining profitability.

Strategies for Success:

- **Pilot Program:** A pilot program for automation was implemented in a specific department, allowing for refinement of the technology and demonstration of its benefits.
- **Employee Involvement:** Employees were involved in the planning and implementation of automation, fostering a sense of ownership and reducing resistance.
- **Comprehensive Training:** A comprehensive training program equipped employees with the necessary skills to operate and maintain the new automated systems.

Result: Global Steel Inc. successfully transitioned to a more automated production process. The new technology improved efficiency and competitiveness, while the training program ensured a smooth skill transfer for the workforce.

Case Study 3: Healthcare System - Ensuring Patient Continuity

Situation: A large hospital underwent a leadership change, with the Chief Medical Officer (CMO) retiring.

Challenges:

- **Maintaining Quality of Care:** Ensuring a smooth transition in leadership without compromising patient care standards.

- **Continuity of Patient Relationships:** Minimizing disruption to ongoing patient treatment plans and doctor-patient relationships.
- **Communication with Staff:** Keeping staff informed about the handover process and the new CMO's vision for the hospital.

Strategies for Success:

- **Overlapping Tenure:** The outgoing and incoming CMOs worked together for several weeks, allowing for knowledge transfer and familiarization with ongoing projects.
- **Patient-Centric Approach:** The handover focused on maintaining continuity of care, with clear communication regarding patient needs and ongoing treatment plans.
- **Staff Town Halls:** The new CMO held town hall meetings to introduce themselves to the staff, discuss

their vision for the hospital, and address any concerns.

Result: The hospital successfully transitioned leadership while maintaining a high standard of patient care. The overlapping tenure ensured knowledge transfer and minimized disruption to ongoing patient treatment plans. Staff felt informed and engaged under the new leadership.

These cases showcase how effective communication, planning, and a commitment to minimizing disruption are key ingredients for a successful handover. By learning from these examples, organizations can navigate their own transitions more effectively, ensuring continuity and paving the way for a successful future.

Chapter 6: Beyond the Handover: Building a Culture of Continuity

Handovers are a crucial but temporary event. They're like a bridge, taking us from one point to the next. But what happens after we cross that bridge? How do we ensure the knowledge, skills, and momentum gained during a handover don't get lost in the shuffle? The answer lies in cultivating a culture of continuity – a way of working that weaves smooth transitions into the very fabric of your organization.

Think of it like this: Imagine your organization as a relay race. Each team member represents a specific function or project. A successful handover is like a flawless baton pass, where the momentum and knowledge are transferred seamlessly. But what if the runners never practiced passing the baton? What if they viewed each leg of the race as an isolated event? Chances are, the race would be a mess, dropping the baton and losing precious time.

Building a culture of continuity is all about practicing those baton passes long before the race even starts. Here's how:

- **Foster a Knowledge-Sharing Mindset:** Encourage open communication and information sharing. This can involve regular team meetings, knowledge-sharing platforms, or even mentorship programs where experienced employees can guide newcomers.
- **Document, Document, Document:** Don't rely solely on people's memories. Create clear, concise documentation that outlines processes, procedures, and best practices. This serves as a valuable resource for existing staff and a springboard for new team members.

- **Embrace Cross-Training:** Encourage employees to learn from each other's roles. This not only creates a more well-rounded workforce but also ensures that critical knowledge isn't siloed within specific individuals.

- **Celebrate Collaboration:** Recognize and reward teamwork and collaboration. This reinforces the idea that success is a collective effort and that everyone is responsible for ensuring the smooth flow of information and expertise.

- **Regular Reviews and Feedback:** Schedule regular check-ins to assess how well knowledge transfer is happening. Encourage feedback from both new and existing team members to identify areas for improvement.

By implementing these practices, you're essentially creating an organizational nervous system where information and knowledge flow freely. This not only makes handovers smoother, but also fosters a sense of collective ownership and responsibility for the organization's success. It's a win-win situation, ensuring a more efficient, adaptable, and future-proof organization.

Remember, a culture of continuity isn't built overnight. It's an ongoing process that requires commitment from leadership and active participation from all team members. But the rewards are significant – a workplace where transitions are seamless, knowledge is readily available, and everyone feels empowered to contribute to the organization's ongoing success. So, ditch the isolated handover mentality and embrace the power of continuity. It's the key to unlocking long-term success in today's ever-changing world.

Chapter 7: The Handover in Different Contexts: A Chameleon Approach

Handovers, like chameleons, need to adapt their approach to blend seamlessly into different environments. While the core principles of communication, planning, and knowledge transfer remain constant, the specifics will vary depending on the context. Let's explore how handovers take shape in various scenarios:

1. Project Handover:

Here, the focus is on transferring project knowledge, deadlines, and ownership of tasks.

- **Key Considerations:** Utilize project management tools, create detailed handover reports outlining project status and risks, and schedule dedicated meetings for clarification and task allocation.

2. Leadership Handover:

This is a high-stakes transition that requires careful planning to ensure continuity of vision and strategy.

- **Key Considerations:** Facilitate meetings between outgoing and incoming leaders, establish clear communication channels, and involve key stakeholders in the handover process.

3. Knowledge Worker Handover:

When an employee departs, their accumulated knowledge needs to be captured and shared effectively.

- **Key Considerations:** Encourage knowledge documentation, conduct exit interviews to capture valuable insights, and leverage knowledge-sharing platforms for ongoing access to expertise.

4. Medical Handover:

Ensuring patient safety is paramount. Clear communication of medical history, medications, and treatment plans is crucial.

- **Key Considerations:** Utilize standardized SBAR (Situation, Background, Assessment, Recommendation) format for clear communication, conduct shift briefings or handover rounds, and prioritize patient well-being throughout the process.

5. Technological Handover:

New systems or software require proper introduction and training for users to avoid disruptions.

- **Key Considerations:** Provide comprehensive user manuals and training materials, schedule hands-on training sessions, and offer ongoing support for troubleshooting and user adoption.

Beyond these specific contexts, consider these additional factors when tailoring your handover strategy:

- **Size and Complexity of the Handover:** A small, well-defined project handover will require less elaborate planning compared to a large-scale leadership transition.
- **Experience Level of the Receiving Party:** Newcomers may require more detailed information and training compared to experienced team members.
- **Organizational Culture:** Open and collaborative cultures will likely have more established knowledge-sharing practices, whereas more siloed environments may require a more structured approach.

By understanding the unique demands of each handover situation and adapting your approach accordingly, you can ensure a smooth transition, minimize disruptions, and pave the way for continued success, regardless of the context. Remember, a well-executed handover isn't just an ending, it's a strong foundation for a new beginning.

The Handover of Leadership: Moses and Joshua

The story of Moses and Joshua in the Bible offers a fascinating case study of leadership handover in an ancient context. Here, the "bridge" we discussed earlier takes the form of a divinely ordained transition from a revered leader to his successor.

Challenges:

- **Moses' Legacy:** Moses was a larger-than-life figure. Stepping into his shoes would be daunting for any successor.

- **Joshua's Experience:** While Joshua was a capable military leader, he lacked Moses' experience in leading a large, diverse group of people for 40 years through the harsh desert.
- **Public Acceptance:** The Israelites might question Joshua's authority and leadership compared to the divinely chosen Moses.

Strategies for Success:

- **Divine Endorsement:** God himself selects Joshua as Moses' successor, publicly endorsing his leadership and providing legitimacy (Numbers 27:18-23).
- **Knowledge Transfer:** Moses mentors Joshua, imparting his wisdom and experience throughout their journey (Exodus 33:11).
- **Gradual Transition:** Joshua already held a leadership position as Moses' "assistant" (Exodus 24:13), allowing for a smoother transition.

- **Public Demonstration:** Moses publicly lays his hands on Joshua, symbolically transferring leadership authority (Deuteronomy 34:9).

Outcomes:

- **Successful Leadership:** Despite the challenges, Joshua proves himself as a capable leader, guiding the Israelites into the Promised Land.
- **Continuity of Vision:** Joshua remains faithful to the mission entrusted to Moses, ensuring the Israelites reach their ultimate goal.

Lessons Learned:

- **Importance of Mentorship:** Investing time in grooming a successor ensures a smooth transition and continuity of knowledge.

- **Public Endorsement:** Building trust and acceptance for the new leader is crucial for a successful handover.
- **Symbolic Rituals:** Symbolic gestures can reaffirm the transfer of power and inspire confidence in the new leader.

While the context of Moses and Joshua's handover is unique, the underlying principles resonate even today. Effective leadership transitions require careful planning, preparation, and a commitment to ensuring the organization's continued success under new guidance. The story serves as a testament to the importance of a well-executed handover, even in extraordinary circumstances.

Chapter 8: Communication Strategies for Complex Handovers - Navigating the Murky Waters.

Complex handovers, like navigating a treacherous river, require clear communication to avoid getting swamped by confusion and delays. This chapter equips you with essential communication strategies to ensure a smooth and successful handover, even in the most challenging situations.

Understanding Complexity:

The first step is recognizing what makes a handover complex. Here are some key factors:

- **Multiple Stakeholders:** A large number of people with diverse interests and needs involved in the handover creates a need for clear and targeted communication.

- **Technical Information:** Complex technical details require careful explanation and a shared understanding of terminology.
- **Uncertainties and Risks:** The presence of unknowns or potential challenges necessitates transparent communication to manage expectations and mitigate risks.
- **Emotional Transitions:** Handovers can be emotionally charged, especially during leadership changes. Sensitive communication is crucial for maintaining morale and trust.

Communication Strategies for Success:

- **Early and Frequent Communication:** Start communication well in advance of the handover, keeping stakeholders informed of the process timeline and key milestones.
- **Multi-Channel Approach:** Utilize various communication channels like meetings, emails,

reports, and knowledge-sharing platforms to cater to different learning styles and preferences.

- **Active Listening:** Practice active listening to ensure understanding and address any concerns or questions promptly.
- **Clear and Concise Language:** Avoid jargon and technical language when possible. Use clear, concise language that everyone can understand, especially when dealing with complex information.
- **Structured Communication Tools:** Leverage tools like standardized handover templates, SBAR (Situation, Background, Assessment, Recommendation) format for medical handovers, or project management dashboards to ensure consistency and clarity in information transfer.
- **Visual Aids:** Utilize visuals like diagrams, flowcharts, or presentations to enhance understanding and retention of complex information.
- **Two-Way Communication:** Encourage two-way communication, allowing the receiving party to ask questions, seek clarification, and provide feedback.

- **Open and Transparent Communication:** Be open and transparent about potential challenges and risks associated with the handover. Honesty builds trust and fosters collaboration.
- **Empathetic Communication:** Acknowledge the emotional aspects of the handover, especially during leadership transitions. Show empathy and understanding to maintain morale and build trust.

Additional Considerations:

- **Cultural Sensitivity:** Be mindful of cultural communication styles when dealing with a diverse group of stakeholders.
- **Confidentiality:** Ensure sensitive information is communicated discreetly through appropriate channels.

This chapter concludes the exploration of handovers. We've covered the challenges, strategies, and different contexts, and finally honed in on communication – the essential ingredient for navigating the sometimes murky waters of complex handovers.

The transition between John the Baptist and Jesus Christ is a fascinating example of a handover with a unique twist. Here's why:

John's Role: The Bridge Builder

John the Baptist wasn't simply a predecessor; he was the herald, the one who prepared the way for Jesus. Imagine John as the bridge builder, constructing a sturdy passage over a roaring river – the expectations and misunderstandings surrounding the Messiah's arrival.

Challenges of the Handover:

- **Shifting Expectations:** John preached a baptism of repentance for the coming judgment. Jesus, however, offered a message of grace and forgiveness. This shift in focus could have confused the people who flocked to John.

- **Discipling Dilemma:** John's disciples initially struggled to understand Jesus' message and role. Some even questioned John about Jesus' identity (John 1:26-28).

- **John's Fading Spotlight:** As Jesus' ministry gained momentum, John's role naturally receded. This could have been a difficult adjustment for John and his followers.

Strategies for a Smooth Transition:

- **John's Public Endorsement:** John publicly declared Jesus as the "Lamb of God" (John 1:29), explicitly directing his followers towards him.
- **Jesus' Acknowledgement:** Jesus recognized John's importance, calling him the "greatest one born among women" (Matthew 11:11).
- **Gradual Shift:** John's imprisonment (Matthew 4:12) coincided with the beginning of Jesus' public ministry, allowing for a gradual handover of attention.

The Outcome: A Fulfilling Transition

While the transition wasn't without its challenges, it ultimately proved successful. John stayed true to his role as the forerunner, diminishing so that Jesus could increase

(John 3:30). His disciples eventually joined Jesus' movement, furthering his mission.

Lessons Learned:

- **Clarity of Purpose:** John's clear understanding of his role as a forerunner helped ensure a smooth transition.
- **Public Acknowledgement:** Public endorsement from the outgoing leader fosters trust and acceptance of the new leader.
- **Gradual Shift:** A gradual handover allows for smoother adaptation for followers of both leaders.

The story of John the Baptist and Jesus Christ reminds us that successful handovers aren't just about efficiency; they're about paving the way for a greater purpose.

Chapter 9: The Long-Term Impact of Effective Handovers - Building Bridges to a Brighter Future

Handovers, often viewed as a one-time event, hold the power to shape the long-term trajectory of an organization. Done effectively, they're not just about transferring information; they're about building bridges to a brighter future. This chapter explores the lasting positive impacts of well-executed handovers.

Benefits of Effective Handovers:

- **Improved Efficiency and Productivity:** Seamless knowledge transfer ensures minimal disruption to ongoing projects and workflows. This translates to quicker onboarding of new team members, improved problem-solving capabilities, and ultimately, increased productivity.

- **Enhanced Quality and Consistency:** Clear communication and proper documentation minimize the risk of errors and ensure consistent adherence to best practices. Imagine a well-maintained bridge allowing for the smooth flow of goods and services – a successful handover creates a similar foundation for quality and consistency.

- **Stronger Team Cohesion and Morale:** When transitions are smooth and communication is open, team members feel valued and supported. This fosters a sense of collaboration, trust, and overall higher morale – crucial ingredients for a thriving team environment.

- **Reduced Risk and Mitigated Challenges:** Anticipating potential issues and establishing clear communication channels allows for proactive problem-solving. This reduces the risk of delays, setbacks, and costly mistakes, just as a sturdy bridge minimizes the risk of accidents during travel.

- **Institutionalized Knowledge and Best Practices:** Effective handovers create a culture of knowledge sharing and documentation. This ensures valuable institutional knowledge doesn't disappear with departing personnel, fostering continuous learning and improvement.
- **Successful Leadership Transitions:** A well-planned handover ensures continuity of vision and strategy during leadership changes. This minimizes disruption and fosters trust in the new leader, paving the way for a smooth and successful transition of power.

Long-Term Impacts:

The positive effects of a successful handover extend far beyond the immediate transition period. They contribute to:

- **A Culture of Continuous Improvement:** By fostering knowledge sharing and open communication, effective handovers create a culture where learning and improvement are ongoing processes. This adaptability allows the organization to stay competitive and thrive in a changing landscape.
- **Stronger Employer Branding:** A reputation for smooth transitions and a commitment to employee development attracts and retains top talent. This positive employer brand becomes a valuable asset in attracting the best and brightest.
- **Enhanced Organizational Resilience:** The ability to navigate transitions effectively makes the organization more resilient in the face of unforeseen changes, such as market fluctuations or personnel turnover. Just as a strong bridge can withstand heavy traffic and harsh weather, an organization with a strong handover culture can weather any storm.

Investing in Handovers:

Handovers may seem like a time-consuming investment, but the long-term benefits outweigh the initial effort. By prioritizing effective handovers, organizations invest in their future, ensuring continued success and a foundation for sustainable growth.

Conclusion:

Effective handovers are more than just a transfer of information; they're a strategic investment in the long-term health and success of an organization. By prioritizing clear communication, knowledge transfer, and a culture of continuous learning, organizations can build bridges to a brighter future, ensuring a smooth and successful journey for everyone involved.

Absolutely, both Joshua and Elisha demonstrate remarkable dedication to staying true to the mission entrusted to them. Here's a breakdown of their strengths and the takeaways for successful leadership transitions:

Joshua:

- **Faithful Execution:** Joshua meticulously followed the instructions laid out by Moses, leading the Israelites to conquer the Promised Land. This highlights the importance of **continuity of vision** when taking over a leadership role.
- **Adaptability:** While remaining faithful to the overall mission, Joshua adjusted strategies based on the evolving situation. This emphasizes the need for **flexibility** and the ability to adapt to changing circumstances while staying true to the core goals.

Elisha:

- **Carrying the Torch:** Elisha inherited the mantle of prophecy from Elijah, continuing to advocate for social justice and adherence to God's teachings. This emphasizes the importance of **preserving core values** during leadership transitions.

- **Building on the Legacy:** Elisha didn't simply replicate Elijah's style; he built upon his predecessor's work, performing miracles and leading the people in new ways. This highlights the importance of **innovation** while staying true to the established mission.

Takeaways for Successful Leadership Transitions:

- **Balance Continuity and Innovation:** New leaders should strive to maintain the core mission and values while also bringing fresh ideas and approaches to the table.
- **Learn from the Past:** Understanding the legacy and strategies of previous leaders provides valuable context for navigating future challenges.
- **Communicate Effectively:** Clear communication with stakeholders ensures everyone is aligned with the vision and mission, both during and after the handover.

- **Adapt to Changing Circumstances:** Flexibility and the ability to adjust strategies based on new situations are crucial for long-term success.

By following these principles, leaders like Joshua and Elisha can ensure a smooth transition and continue to guide their organizations towards achieving their goals. Their dedication to the mission and their ability to adapt while staying true to core values serve as inspiring examples for future leaders.

Chapter 10: The Future of Leadership Handovers - A Glimpse into a Smoother Tomorrow.

The landscape of leadership handovers is on the cusp of a transformative era. As technology evolves and our understanding of human potential deepens, we can expect a future brimming with possibilities for smoother, more impactful transitions. Here's a glimpse into what the exciting possibilities the future holds:

Technological Advancements:

- **AI-Powered Mentorship:** Imagine intelligent AI systems that analyze an outgoing leader's communication style, decision-making processes, and leadership philosophies. This data could then be used to create personalized mentorship programs for incoming leaders, fostering a virtual mentor who adapts to their individual learning needs.
- **Big Data and Predictive Analytics:** By leveraging vast datasets on leadership styles, team dynamics, and past handover successes and failures, organizations could utilize predictive analytics to identify potential challenges and recommend tailored handover strategies. This would be akin to using weather forecasts to prepare for a journey, allowing for proactive steps to mitigate risks.

- **Blockchain-Secured Knowledge Transfer:** Blockchain technology, known for its secure and transparent data storage, could be harnessed to create tamper-proof repositories of institutional knowledge. This would ensure the secure transfer of critical information and intellectual property during handovers, minimizing the risk of loss or alteration.

Evolving Practices:

- **Focus on Diversity, Equity, and Inclusion (DE&I):** The future of handovers will likely prioritize fostering a culture of DE&I. This could involve creating diverse mentor pools, developing culturally sensitive handover strategies, and ensuring equitable access to leadership development opportunities for all potential successors.
- **Reverse Mentoring Programs:** In addition to traditional top-down knowledge transfer, reverse mentoring programs could see incoming leaders mentor outgoing leaders in areas like new technologies or emerging market trends. This fosters a two-way flow of knowledge and ensures both parties remain adaptable and relevant.
- **Gamification and Interactive Learning:** Gamified learning platforms and interactive simulations can transform handover training into an engaging and immersive experience. Imagine

leadership handover training that feels like playing a challenging and rewarding video game, promoting knowledge retention and skill development.

A Collaborative Future:

As with any successful endeavor, the future of leadership handovers is a collaborative effort. Here are some key players involved:

- **Leadership Development Specialists:** These specialists will become architects of the future, designing data-driven handover programs that leverage cutting-edge technology and incorporate the latest findings in neuroscience and leadership psychology.
- **Organizational Psychologists:** By understanding the human aspects of transitions, psychologists can help design handovers that minimize stress, promote emotional intelligence, and foster trust between outgoing and incoming leaders.
- **Change Management Experts:** Experts in navigating organizational change will be crucial in guiding teams through the emotional and cultural shifts that often accompany leadership transitions.
- **Outgoing and Incoming Leaders:** The cornerstone of any successful handover remains the active participation of both leaders. A spirit of

collaboration, open communication, and a willingness to learn from each other will be paramount for a smooth and successful transition.

The Bottom Line:

By embracing these advancements and fostering a collaborative spirit, organizations can transform handovers from a logistical hurdle into a strategic catalyst for growth. The future of leadership handovers holds immense potential to create a more dynamic, adaptable, and future-proof landscape for organizations of all sizes. Ultimately, the key remains the same: a commitment to clear communication, knowledge transfer, and a focus on continuous learning. With these elements in place, organizations can unlock the full potential of their leadership pipeline, ensuring a thriving future for generations to come.[2]

---

[2]

Conclusion: The Power of Effective Handovers - A Legacy of Smooth Transitions.

Throughout this book, we've explored the complexities and nuances of navigating leadership handovers. We've delved into the challenges of transferring knowledge, managing emotions, and ensuring continuity during periods of change. But more importantly, we've painted a vivid picture of the immense potential that effective handovers hold.

Handovers are not merely logistical hurdles; they are strategic opportunities to bridge the gap between past, present, and future. By prioritizing clear communication, meticulous planning, and a commitment to knowledge transfer, organizations can transform handovers into springboards for growth and innovation.

The future of leadership handovers is brimming with exciting possibilities. Technological advancements promise a more streamlined and personalized handover experience. Collaborative efforts between leadership development specialists, psychologists, and change management experts will ensure a well-rounded approach that addresses both the technical and human aspects of transitions.

Ultimately, the success of any handover hinges on a fundamental principle: a focus on people. Effective handovers not only ensure continuity of leadership but also empower individuals. They provide outgoing leaders with a sense of legacy and purpose, while equipping incoming leaders with the knowledge, skills, and confidence to thrive in their new roles.

The journey of effective handovers is an ongoing symphony, requiring a well-rehearsed orchestra of leaders, specialists, and collaborators. By embracing a spirit of continuous learning, innovation, and collaboration, organizations can cultivate a culture where handovers are not just endured, but celebrated. This, in turn, paves the way for a future where leadership transitions are seamless, leaders are well-prepared, and organizations are empowered to reach their full potential.

As we conclude this exploration, let the lessons learned throughout this book serve as a guiding melody. By prioritizing effective handovers, organizations can ensure a legacy of smooth transitions, empowered leaders, and a thriving future for generations to come. Remember, a well-orchestrated handover is not just the end of one chapter, but the exciting beginning of the next.